Empty Places
Poems for the Lost

Issara Simone Edwards

Copyright © 2024 by Issara Simone Edwards

All rights reserved. This book or any portion thereof may not be reproduced or used in any manner, except for brief quotations in a book review, without prior written permission from the author and publisher.

Published 2024

Book design by Issara Simone Edwards

Illustrations by Issara Simone Edwards

Contents

This Poem 3

The Fox and the Cat 6

Longing 9

There's Never Nowhere to Go 11

Monster (Part I) 13

Monster (Part II) 16

Monster (Part III) 18

Monster (Part IV) 21

Love is Only Affected by Time 24

Red Rose 26

The Last Oyster Shell 28

Graffiti on Bathroom Walls 30

Message in a Bottle 32

Touch 34

My Mother's Daughter 36

Lost Boy 39

Blackbird 42

Daughter 44

Across the Earth 47

The Things I Want to Do 49

A Dream 51

A SPace 54

Alone With You	56
Sea Stone, River Tumbled	58
Eternal	61
White Feather	63
Baby Names	65
Cling to My Skin	67
All the songs we sing are to ourselves	69
Witch	71
Oh, Freesia	74
Sheep are lambs who have forgotten how to leap	77
Surrender	80
Sweet Waters	82
Bird Watching on a Grey Evening	84
Same	86
The Art Collection	88
The Surrealist	90
Sweet Friend	92
King of Pens	94
Words and Poets	96
Dad's Car	98
Leave me Here	100
In My Little World	103
Be My Body	106
Shibari	108

It's not always damage….. 111
Séance 113
Remind Me... 115
Grandfather Clock... 117
In the Infinity of a Wolf Moon.. 119
Should Have Started.. 122
A Thought in a Hundred Parts… 123

These poems are to be read and not spoken aloud.

Let them remain in your mind, let them open doors to new worlds

Empty Places

Empty Places

This Poem

I wrote my first poem in a tiny classroom on a tiny hill,

And marvelled at the way the world fell around it.

It joined the pantheon of short stories I'd written,

Of the novels I would write,

And in my mind, there was no difference between any of them.

A kid in school said 'eww' when she saw me writing poetry,

And I thought, 'how small your world must be',

But felt the condemnation of it settle in,

When all around her seemed to agree.

My English teacher told me poetry should be kept as a hobby,

With a nod as he gave me a B+,

Joining the choir of family and friends, teachers and mentors,

Who'd recite the holy mantra, 'you can't make a living from writing'.

My editor told me he won't publish poetry,

The world is already too thick with it,

I'm better off writing a novel, or a series of novels,

The money is in the serial.

Sometimes I think, 'if the world is so thick with poetry,

Then surely there's a demand for it?'

But I understand the meaning behind his words,

A poem can't stand out in a crowd,

An unknown voice can't be heard in a din.

You're better off self-publishing, friends and fellow writers tell me,

Not understanding the validation that I need

For my silly little hobby, for my disgusting, shameful crime,

For my waste of words and paper.

Not understanding that it's all the same to me,

That I still don't see the difference,

A short story, a novel, a poem,

Why is one worth more than another?

Empty Places

The Fox and the Cat

On one very stormy night I saw a fox sat on a bench,
Sheltering under a tree,
Sat quite calmly next to it was a small black cat.
It was such an odd sight that although the wind raged,
And rain fell down in icy sheets, lightning shattered the sky,
The fox and the cat held me.
The cat looked nervous, glancing, every now and then,
With darting, sideways eyes at the fox.
The storm had forced them to seek shelter together,
But the cat still seemed far from trusting.
The fox seemed at ease, if not a little mischievous.
Every now and again he would twitch, just slightly,
In the unsettled cat's direction.
The cat would flinch, body poised to run,
It's fur bristling with tension.
If I didn't know better, I'd swear the fox was teasing him,
And greatly enjoying each moment.
The scene didn't end with the resting of the storm, or a civil parting of ways,
But with one huge lurch from the fox, a pounce towards the cat.
Maybe he'd had enough of sharing his shelter, maybe he just couldn't resist.

The cat, deciding the storm was better than possible death,

Ran out into the wind and rain, as the fox sat back.

His tail flicked, he became still and peaceful, with an expression on his small face

That looked very much like, 'What was that guy's problem?'

Empty Places

Longing

It's summer, and I find myself…

Not yearning, but waiting…

Eagerly awaiting autumn and the falling of leaves.

The familiarity of barrenness, spindly trees and black branches

Under ashy clouds that constantly threaten rain.

I find that instead of enjoying the thrill of sun and heat,

The swell of warmth and the tan on my skin,

I'm reminiscent of chill, of cold that burns cheeks,

Of fake fur hoods and wellington boots,

Damp, dead leaves and the emerald of evergreens that refuse to dim.

Instead of ice cream in summer,

I want ice cream in winter.

Frothy, stirred up in my favourite mug,

Not melting down the side of a cone.

I want chapped lips and cold toes,

Frost on the windows and tealights illuminating gloom.

I want pumpkin spiced everything,

Marshmallows in cocoa

And a sweet smell in the air like it might just snow.

And when the first leaves fall, and the nights get colder,

I'll say: 'Do you remember when it was summer?

Will it ever be warm again?

Empty Places

There's Never Nowhere to Go

Meet me under the stars and be weird with me,

And I'll tell you the dream I had about you.

I'll confess my ideas,

And share with you my wishes.

I'll open up the sky, fold back the clouds

And fill the world with you.

So, meet me under the stars, and be weird with me.

Empty Places

Monster (Part I)

It's been a while, since I've done this,

Trace the lines of your veins, feel the pulse under my fingers.

Holding a shell up to my ear,

The sound of waves becoming mine.

My head on your chest, the beat to live a life by,

My life by.

Trying to remember who I was before,

Vague images of innocence and childish wonder.

The transformations I've endured,

Constricted myself into,

To win you, to keep you, to own you.

What have I become to be yours?

A love thread through time,

A love wrapped around words and perpetuating ideals.

An imaginary love, glistening like fairy lights.

Your arms around me only echoes of my arms around you.

You hid your secrets in words you borrowed.

You quoted love songs and spoke them like vows,

Filling your mouth with poetry that never travelled to heart or eyes.

Do you see me, am I as much illusion to you now

As I was fantasy then?

What have I become to be yours?

How did I become this monster?
You'll never know what it takes from me,
Sleeping in the bed with you that once felt like home,
But now feels cold and alien.
You'll never know how many nights I've held screams in my mouth,
Razors in my fists.
Is the only way out of this your end or mine?
Will I love you any more or less tomorrow?

Empty Places

Monster (Part II)

The ring on my finger, so loose it slips over skin like water.
Sliding away, the fluttering pages of a conscience,
Torn from its spine, cast into waters to drown.
Solidity vanishing, sinking lower under gasps for breath.
A stone heart dropped in an ocean where no diver can retrieve it.
It's not something I need anymore,
It's a love that's replaceable, like everything else,
As replaceable as hope and loss.
Am I the monster you've made me out to be?
Humanity sleeping beneath the surface of the villain you've cast me as.
Traitor, betrayer, liar, sinner,
I'll collect them as badges, names to call myself by.
I'll make myself into your myth, your monster, your nightmares,
And rage against the world,
Protecting you from all the demons lurking in it,
I'll be their worst fear as well as yours.
And when the world wants to consume you, I'll fight with all I have,
Because even without you in my life,
I'll do all I need to keep you.

Empty Places

Monster (Part III)

You've nowhere left to hide.

If I'm the villain, I'm the villain

And I'm hunting me down.

There's nothing else that seems to quell this hunger,

A look from her, a look from you,

A memory of running towards you,

Replaced by those of running from.

There's something inside me that'll eat you alive.

Your heart hits like a drum,

My heart hunts for fun.

Every mistake I made, I made yours.

Using algebra and plot twists to rewrite my own life.

Crossing lines and breaking boundaries,

Playing at the edges of what's clever

To indulge in the dark.

Your heart hitting like a drum,

My heart hurting you for fun.

The monster under your bed,

Your blood still on my tongue.

Playing the part I claimed for myself so well,

Letting fear of myself be me.

What's left underneath it all?

We'll be monsters together,

Hiding away from our sins.

Empty Places

Monster (Part IV)

On a fallen star burning away the night,

My fingers in my mother's hand,

Making a wish that my face would never change.

May my eyes always be curious,

My features soft,

My expression open,

My mouth loving.

May I not become hard and harsh,

May the stone inside not show on my face.

Looking through photos,

The changing face in the mirror,

The reflection of time,

An aging star fading under the night.

Bones under skin,

Dark pebbles over closed eyes,

A coin over blistered lips.

Skeletal scarecrow searching for the child

Who held their mothers hand and made a wish.

Did I let them do this to me?

Did I turn myself into a monster?

Trying to erase it,

Rose hip oil under the eyes,

beeswax on the lips,

A smile,

A nonchalant expression.

Inside a desire to tear the world apart,

To feel its ribs crack under my fingers.

I can paint my nails and brush my hair,

An illusion of togetherness.

The ring on my finger a mockery of love,

The breasts under my shirt burning

Under the cross around my neck.

This is who I am now.

This is all I am now.

The warning sign at the end of the dock,

The monster crawling away from the light.

Empty Places

Love is Only Affected by Time

Lying in the same bed, they could be miles apart.

He lies still, pretending to sleep,

Waiting for her to understand him the way she used to.

She lies still, pretending to sleep,

Waiting for him to reach out, call her name,

Touch her the way he used to.

He waits for her to trust him with all her deepest thoughts,

The way she used to.

She waits for him to say, 'I love you',

With the same conviction he once had.

He wishes she would accept

That he doesn't feel what he once did for her.

She wishes to feel his kiss on the nape of her neck.

He longs to wake up alone,

Not in bed with a stranger every morning.

She longs to be with the man she married,

Not the bloating sham he's turning into.

He wants nothing more than for her to say she's leaving him for good.

She wants nothing more than for him to say he'll never leave her.

Every night they wonder how they got so far apart,

When their love was meant to last forever.

Empty Places

Red Rose

I found you growing in a graveyard, soft to the touch, like velvet, like soft skin, smelling sweetly of decay.

I bruised you walking home, held you tightly between fingers and thumb, too scared to lose you in the wind.

I followed a path of silver birches to find you, you mark the start of something, a new journey, a new beginning.

Empty Places

The Last Oyster Shell

Oyster shells,

Blue lace shuffled across open sky,

A feeling of being lifted.

'Stop worrying about money' she says 'and breathe.'

So, I put the oyster shell on a shelf in my room,

Smelling faintly of ashes, a little acrylic melted on its surface,

A part of the collection now.

It'll sit next to a Bast statuette, and a drawing of a seedless pomegranate.

Empty Places

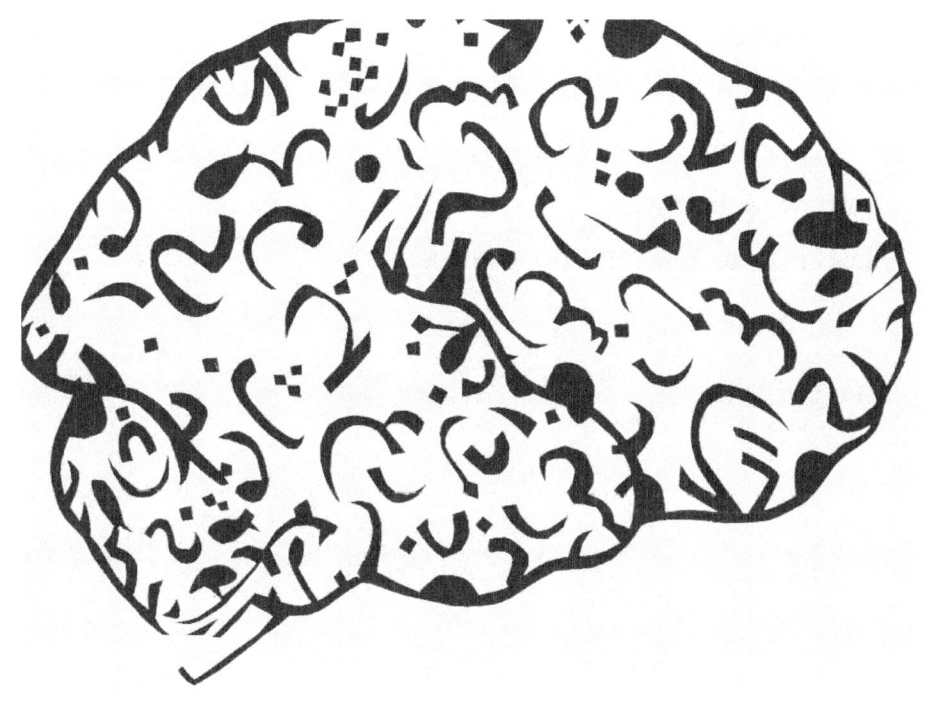

Graffiti on Bathroom Walls

Diaries are fragmented recollections,

A journal of disjointed remembering.

Personality becomes graffiti on bathroom walls,

Expectation and modes painted on to us.

A shy child echoes through a home,

A love, dreamt, that is world ending.

A tiny red bird remembered as a burst of colour in the snow.

Ripe, juicy fruit, an over-ripe peach,

Overflowing at a touch.

I don't recognise myself in you anymore.

Empty Places

Message in a Bottle

Footsteps in the sand.

I have a necklace that I've never worn.

I bought it because it reminded me of a witch's talisman,

And I wanted it to be mine.

I look at it now, hanging on the wall,

And it looks like a letter in a bottle.

A lost relic, floating around in a vast ocean,

Black seaweed tangled around it,

A message still waiting to be read.

I'm so good at not finishing things.

But I like the stillness here, the rain,

The quiet it creates.

Empty Places

ck and connected.
it felt like the retelling of a
how alike they are, knitting and stitch
a yarn, weaving a ale.

wet, and I'm moving, I dreamt that I was on a at,
ating across the bottom of the sea, the current was
ing me along. When I opened my eyes, I was in a four
the bobbing of the waves was just the mattress
ancing under the eight of my tossing and ing.
s dark, just the odd sh t f m a candle
ghting. I'm not here alo I hould be afraid, but I
like I'm aming, nothin ing
s happe can handle le
n I wak e up, I'll
eyes, o lose them, s
from me, p light etch
Is there a city out there? h world? Or is it just
oned in nowhere? Are the lights I keep seeing
ildings, streetlights, are y more like
ld Christmas lights on a dark tree?
ll sleep when I hear rustling on t he
ang utlery, the pouring of l Th
bed squeeze my eyes shut a my
ow fa hat looks, force myself to eathe
, sleeping breath . The creak g stops just
eathing, I keep my eyes closed. The creaki

case. There's breakfast on the
t looks like orange ju

33

Touch

I want to be seen, to be seen, I want you to see me.

I want fingers, fingers inside my mouth, inside my eyes,

Pulling back lids, pulling back my mind.

This is another sleepless night,

This is another revenge porno for you.

I want to twist the knife; I want to feel it clawing down my spine.

And I try, I've tried to phase you out,

But you're in, you're in my blood.

I want to be seen, to be seen,

I want you to see my scream and fake and fake you out.

I want touch, to be touched, hands raking my skin

Until all I feel is numb inside.

This is another sleepless night,

This is another curse I can't take back.

I want to tame my mind,

But its rage is pure and fuels this fight.

I want to chase you out,

But it's too late, too late, you've made your mark.

I want to fill this void, but in truth,

I like the space you've left behind.

Empty Places

My Mother's Daughter

I am my mother's daughter,
I strip down to skin and that's all I see.
I am my mother's daughter,
My fear is inherited,
A pendulum that swings out further and further,
Back and forth through generations.
I am my mother's daughter,
I am the fear she placed in me.

I have cared for this fear, nurtured it, cultivated it.
I have never laughed at it or chided it,
I've loved and protected it.
It in turn has whispered, shrieked and bellowed.
It's protected me, kept beasts at bay,
Or so it says.

I am my mother's daughter,
I am a black woman born into a world
Where neither of these things are valued.
I am my mother's daughter,
I am the fears given to me and held onto by me.
I am all my failures and all of hers,

I am all the blame she has taken and all the blame I have given.

No one told me to hold these fears so tight,
To fold them into my bones and blood.
Only I can take the blame for that,
Only I can fix this generational hurt.
Only I can walk the history in my blood,
The maze, the labyrinth at the centre of it all.

I am my father's daughter.
I see it in my eyes, my hands, my feet, the texture of my skin.
I am my father's daughter, a rusted pair of scissors, used but still sharp,
Cutting any visible thread of connection with the ease of breathing in and out.

I am my father's daughter,
A disconnection from self and feeling,
From anything or anyone that can break me.
I am the lies I tell, to myself and others,
The booze that numbs the pain and the music that drowns it out.
I am giving up and giving in,
I am the child they made.

Empty Places

Lost Boy

I would be a lost boy,

Wafer thin and sharp like glass.

My words would roll like silken eels,

Charms and curses would cut from my lips,

Cracked and dry as they may be.

My tongue would twist out truths and lies,

And I'd dare anyone to tell one from the other.

I would be a wanderer,

A dodger on the streets.

My rough bare feet, split heels and splintered toes

Would dance around brogues, cleets and clogs,

Espadrilles, boots, sandals and trainers.

I'd be unknown, a glint, a shadow,

A memory faded long ago.

A breeze passing by.

Yes, I would be a lost boy,

A deserter on an ageless island.

I'd carve out sand huts and live like a hermit.

I'd spend my days in trees, watching creatures come and go.

I'd be simple and wild always looking for a place to call home.

Empty Places

I'd be half mad from weeping,

And half sane from peace.

I'd be a lost boy,

Stretched across the surface,

A map with a single black spot.

Empty Places

Blackbird

There's a spell, in a bottle, in a cauldron, burning bright.
There's a spell, in a crystal, in scented oils, in herbs and stones.
There's a spell, caught in weavings, the webs of a dreamcatcher,
And the spell is a blackbird calling.

There's a spell in an obelisk of tiger's eye and pyrite,
Holding confidence and a boost of strength.
There's a spell with an egg, with a serpent in it,
A joining of opposing forces that make a whole.

There's a spell in a Serph stone and a cupid's arrow,
Heavy with sex and stimulated with power.
There's a spell in the child created, in the hearts that fit together,
In the souls that reach for each other across wide spaces.

There's a spell with fire in it, with smoke and water and gifts.
There's love, that's the word for it, there's love in this room.

Empty Places

Daughter

I watched a movie today,

Too terrible to mention by name,

Too embarrassing to claim.

Yet less than twelve minutes in

I was on my knees in tears,

Like a Catholic awaiting absolution.

The scene in the movie, a father and his daughter.

The words that came from his mouth,

'Why do you have to be so selfish?'

His daughter hadn't done anything that I would note as 'selfish',

She had only asked to be herself

And not be what he wanted.

In his eyes, his world, was duty and appearance.

In her eyes, her world, was honouring herself and her truth.

But his words struck as though they were aimed at me directly,

Because for so long and by so many, these words have been.

I'd already accepted my selfishness,

From five years old I've been told what I am.

The words used not as a weapon to hurt me,

But as a firm hand to mould me into shape.

Can I call this failure to be 'selfless' there's or mine?

To this day, I'd rather be myself than conform to another's idea.

Empty Places

I've owned my title and accepted my status,

So why does the word still hurt?

Long after the movie has ended,

Why are the words still haunting?

Does it hurt because it hit truth,

Or because it struck something deeper?

Does it hurt because I realise now

That I was never the selfish one?

Does it hurt because after thirty-six years,

I realise what love is?

Real love isn't trying to change someone

Into what they should be.

Real love is accepting them for who they are.

Empty Places

Across the Earth

I'm divided, too many people all at once,

In too many worlds at once.

My body is a landscape, a prison, a white rose,

Fragile of colour and petal,

A craving of openness,

The vulnerability of touch,

The secrecy of motherhood,

The burden of wings.

Outnumbered by my selves and in the dark,

I'm too many people, all at once.

Empty Places

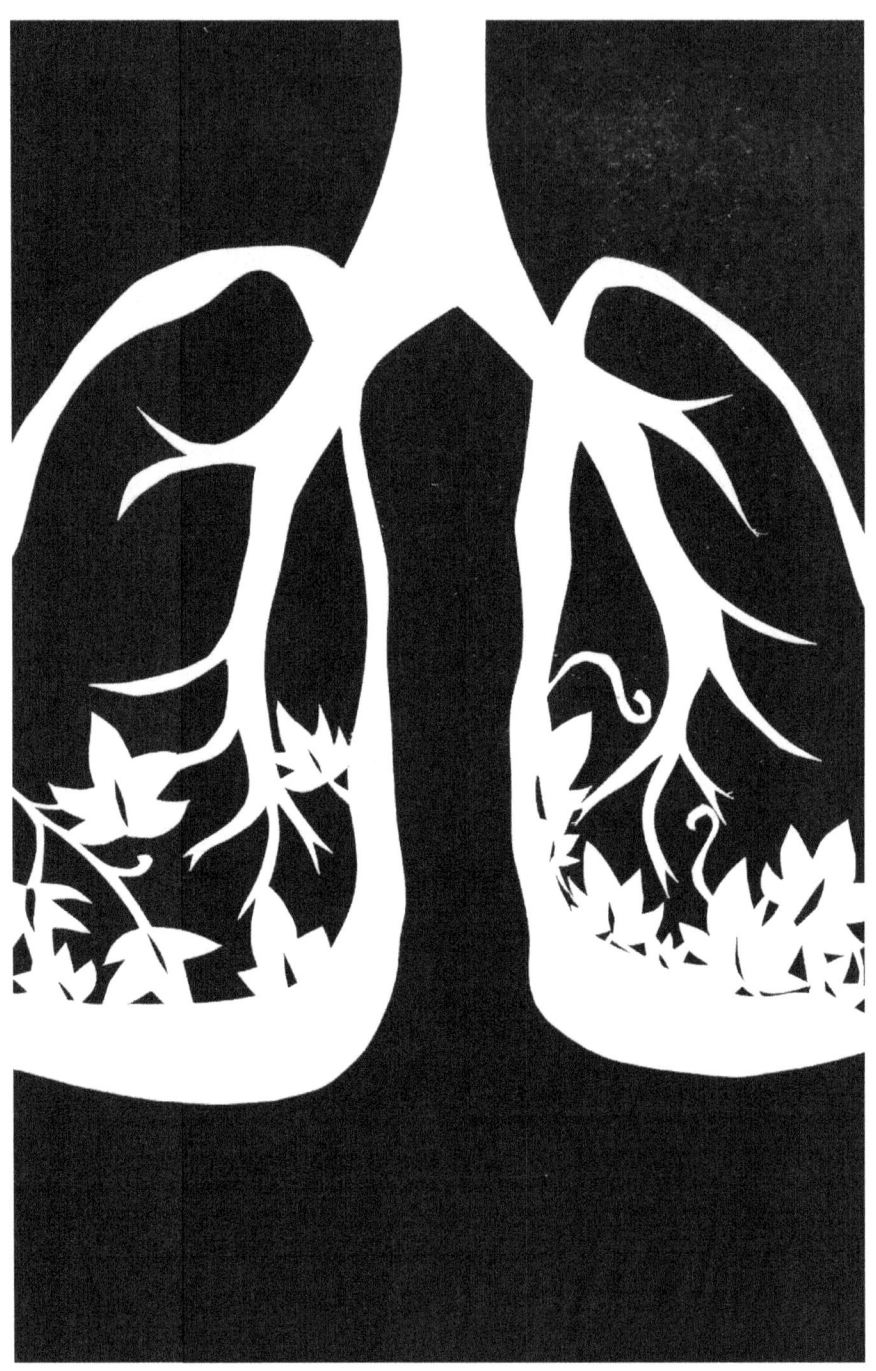

The Things I Want to Do

Change the water in the oil burner

Paint a nightingale with a red eye

Take the pile of clothes off the floor

And put them away all tidy in draws.

Change the carpet in the bedroom

Get a plumber to fix the leaky tap

Have someone work the knots out of my shoulders

Shave under my arms and wash my hair

Getoutofbedgetoutofbedgetoutofbed

Drink a glass of water

Feel hopeful

Check my messages and pick up my phone

Speak to another person and mean the words I say

Not flinch from your touch

Not jump at every sound

Make pancakes

Step outside

Feel okay, just, okay.

Empty Places

A Dream

I want a woman with a voice like THC

A voice to curl up in

A voice that settles in the stomach

And stirs my thoughts like storm clouds.

I want a woman who calls me King

Who fits into me and lets me reign

Who can carry me and herself too.

I want a woman to kneel before

Who takes me to her bed

And let's her body sing me to sleep

Who opens to me

Unfolds and pearls like melting ice cream.

I want a woman who looks like a sci-fi queen

A ghetto sister, an Asian babe,

A voodoo angel, a gothic daughter,

an elven princess, a comic book icon.

I want a woman who loves me

I want a woman to love.

I want a confidante, a partner in crime,

An equal.

I want forever, a myth made real.

I want a dream,

I want a lot.

Empty Places

A SPace

There's _ time _ here, _ there's _ a _ space, _ there's _ openness.
There's _ a _ between, _ a _ space _ for _ roaming.
The _ messenger _ creeping _ backwards _ and _ the
Expansion _ of _ a _ will.
There's _ a _ space _ between _ words _ and _ thought _ and _ action,
A _ stillness _ between _ two _ points _ and _ the
Movement _ in _ between _ them.
There's _ a _ resentment _ in _ me _ for _ having _ to _ speak,
To _ convey _ ideas _ and _ meaning _ in _ words
When _ I _ feel _ beyond _ them,
The _ heaviness _ of _ them, _ the _ stock _ motion _ of _ them.
Then _ I _ remember, _ there's _ space _ here,
A _ space_ to _ learn _ and _ grow,
To _ expand _ beyond _ my _ limits.
There's _ lost _ tales _ here, _ and _ pasts _ explored _ as _ time.
So _ I _ creep _ backwards _ and _ let _ myself _ expand
Into _ the _ spaces _ left _ behind.
I _ count _ the_ words _ I _ use, _ their _ meanings, _ and _ their _ names.
I _ reprise_ their _ roles, _ and _ use _ them _ all _ again.

Empty Places

Alone With You

What happens when you're alone?

When I'm alone, there's an expanse, a release.

I spread out among the empty spaces around me.

I'm not a collection of atoms compressed into a single being anymore,

I become the particles in the air, everything at once.

I put on The Scream, by Siouxsie and the Banshees

And let the eternity of me drift as the record spins.

Content, for the moment, that it isn't quite enough.

For now, I can still feel the sinew of flesh and the gravity of bone.

For now, I'm still here, but splintered

Across all time and all worlds.

Empty Places

Sea Stone, River Tumbled

Calculating the distance between fear and hubris,
I scrub the soles of my feet with sand and salt.
Soft waves rippling under me,
Washing away dead skin.
Wet and open, parting my thighs to place a stone,
A crystal of form and light.
My body is condensed, moments piled on top each other,
I carry each one.
In this cocoon of myself I resist the wide-open spaces
Until night draws in.
In the dark the openness is lessened, muted,
The space heavier and compact.
I fit inside it like a sliver of light.
In the dark I can be the moon, shimmering, silver, pale,
And I can be the sun,
A ray of yellow, red and gold.
I can be two feathers bound with a bead.
I can be the top of a mountain
Looking out at vast seas.
In a moment between moments, I can be
All these things,
A question and an answer,

Empty Places

A loneliness reaching too deep to pull out.

I can let the salt and sand tattoo me,

This will be its parting gift,

A cross at the edge of my eye,

To show me where the tides have come and gone.

I let the stone sink into the water,

And let all I am go with it.

For the love of moving backwards,

For the love of all that remains unseen,

In me and in you.

Empty Places

Eternal

A story told in pieces

Evolving consciousness

Development of form and thought

The fabric and architecture of reality

We are not the ones left behind anymore

The archaic hold onto the structures of old

Let them fall behind

We are the ones with visions in our eyes

The embrace of new ideas

We are the eternal cycle

Revolutions upon revolutions

The fire burning without end

Empty Places

White Feather

I am not my body.

I have known that when sleep takes me,

I am more myself without this form.

I am not the ideas you place on me.

I have known, as I know now,

The restrictions of your expectations.

I am not the clothes I wear.

I know that the clothes don't make the man or the woman,

They're toys to flatter children.

I am not my gender or the promises made by it.

I am whoever I will to be,

This is a reminder to myself as well as you.

Empty Places

Baby Names

We have journeys to go on and paths to walk

Mysteries to learn and riddles to solve.

We have new soils to feel under our feet

And new acquaintances to make.

There are new roots to stumble over,

New mistakes and missteps.

We have lineages to recover

And old patterns to break.

If we can be who we are without settling,

If we can be who we are in worlds that try to reshape us,

If we can fill in the blanks of our lives,

Then no power in the universe can stop us.

Empty Places

Cling to My Skin

I'm happy here in my decision.

I feel grounded in it,

Secure and sturdy in it.

I fear regret of it.

Standing outside,

The night air a film of frost around me,

I can feel that fear and not be guided by it.

My body begins to shiver,

But the cold alleviates my mind of burdens.

I can do this.

I can choose this path I'm walking,

And remain stubbornly fixed to it.

I can do anything here.

And anything is what I choose.

Empty Places

All the songs we sing are to ourselves

I will keep you in roses.
Even though the ground is frozen over,
I will water the soil until steam rises and frost thaws.
I will place fur rugs beneath your feet to keep them warm,
Collect your tears in a bowl and fill your heart with honey.
I will keep you in roses.
I will trim the thorns and gild the leaves,
Dry them in the rafters so they freeze in time.
I will place kisses in the palms of your hands,
And draw patterns over the scars.
I will write messages into each step I take,
So that you know, you're never alone.

Empty Places

Witch I

I am unknown.

I live in unknown places,

Under barnacles at the bottom of the sea,

Behind giant clouds in the shape of castles.

I sneak out at night,

On overcast or misty days,

To skulk through undergrowth,

Or to peek down from the tops of trees.

I can remain unseen, even in plain view.

There are some days where you can pass right through me,

And others where I'm merely a bump on the road.

I have an unrecognisable spirit, an ever-changing heart,

And eyes that see into other worlds.

I could whisper my name to you,

And you would hear it as a mystery,

A thing of familiarity, a thing almost remembered.

You'll say, 'there was someone I used to know,

But now I can't even recall if it was real.'

I am unknown.

I live in unknown places,

Inhabit unknown thoughts, dreams and fables.

Empty Places

I'm the ghost you've seen out of the corner of your eye,

A memory of a dream that someone else had.

I'm a story you once heard,

I'm the stranger in a photograph, you don't remember taking.

Empty Places

Oh, Freesia

Oh, Freesia,

My mother had a friend,

Who would visit from time to time.

She'd bring gifts,

Books on astrology, crystals and tarot cards.

Oh, Freesia,

Speak of lasting friendship.

She'd talk to me about indigo children and celestine prophecies,

About how we were all evolving into higher states.

Oh, Freesia,

Speak of lasting friendship and summer flowers.

Until one day, she disappeared.

No more visits, no phone calls,

Silence and empty space on the sofa.

Oh, Freesia,

Speak of lasting friendship, summer flowers and thoughtfulness.

My mother would ask about her,

Stopping her children in the street to check if she was okay.

Oh, Freesia,

Speak of lasting friendship, summer flowers, thoughtfulness and trust.

After years of silence, one day she knocked,

Perched on the sofa, a bird eager to fly.

Oh, Freesia,

Speak of lasting friendship, summer flowers, thoughtfulness, trust and love.

She said. 'I'm still alive!', with a strangers, pensive smile.

What went unsaid, in the minutes she remained, was,

'This is the goodbye I didn't give before. Stop asking about me. I've moved on.'

Oh, Freesia,

Speak of lasting friendship, summer flowers, thoughtfulness, trust, love and innocence.

Is this all we are?

People who orbit in and out of each other's lives?

Friends for a moment and then strangers in the next?

Oh, Freesia,

Speak of lasting friendship, summer flowers, thoughtfulness, trust, love and innocence.

Oh, Freesia,

Speak of us, and what we will become.

Empty Places

Sheep are lambs who have forgotten how to leap

I wanted more of you tattooed on me.

Before my skin got worn,

My temperament to fearful.

I wanted every word you ever said,

And every promise you ever made

To decorate my body,

A road map of a life explored.

I wanted to mess with the frequency of time

To be with you again,

Rewrite my dreams to match your idea

Of who I should be.

I wanted to stay still for you,

Remain in a place you could find me,

Fixed at an age you'd remember,

At the stage of forming and reforming,

A place where thought and ideas had flight.

But with each mirror held up,

I've changed under its glare.

I've become an echo of who I was,

A person you would barely recognise.

What am I now in the light of it all,

A lost spell, I forgot to preserve?

We were all possibility before we grew up,

Now we can barely remember what it was to leap.

Empty Places

Surrender

It doesn't matter if I fall, the earth has got my back.

She can hold me up when I can't,

Support me with her many limbed trees,

Soften my landings with her cushioned soil,

Wrap me up in the tenderness of her touch.

It doesn't matter if I lose control,

If I feel defeated under the weight of the world,

If I can't keep my head above water.

The sea is where we were born, and our bodies remember it well.

We can learn to breathe underwater,

Go in and out with the tide, move with the flow of rivers,

Our mother won't let us drown.

It doesn't matter if I fail at this,

The world will still keep turning.

I'll learn, I'll grow, I'll remember I surrendered,

To my own will, and my own design.

There will be new paths to walk,

New streams to swim in.

I only have to remind myself,

I'm never as alone as I think.

Empty Places

Sweet Waters

I snuggle down into the burrow of myself

And let my breath cocoon me.

Liquorice on my lips, roots around each finger,

Indulging in the taste of salt, I let the tears come

And a crow passes overhead.

I'll water this garden with honey and make the waters sweet,

The rest will be inside myself.

Until my time here is complete,

This is where you'll find me,

All snug and under the sky,

Until a crow passes back this way.

Empty Places

Bird Watching on a Grey Evening

Have you ever watched birds fly?

They say they only have to watch the one in front,

To follow its direction, to stay in formation.

Others say it's a trick we'll never understand,

A murmuration in the brain,

A psychic link of feather and thread between each bird.

I want to believe your first thought,

You only have to watch the bird in front of you.

We only have to know what's right in front of us,

To not get lost in the clouds.

Empty Places

Same

If I told you I was a little lost,

Would that be okay?

If I told you I wake up in the middle of the night,

Feeling confused and uncertain,

Would you know what to say?

If I told you there are days when I miss being touched,

Would you find it in you to hold me?

If I told you I'm scared to die unfinished,

Would you tell me you feel the same?

Empty Places

The Art Collection

This book of fairy tales stains my fingers black with ink.

It wants to leave a part of itself with me.

I want to reproduce each picture,

Change them from black and white to colour,

From block, ink etchings, to Japanese prints.

All pinks and blues and swirling waters.

Cold feet and cold skin,

I surround myself with art and found objects,

Objects that will outlast me,

Or be burned in a fire on my grave.

Empty Places

The Surrealist

Watching the sunrise through the window of a van
That is parked in front of the window of my house.
At which point does the sunrise become unreality,
A hyper-reality being viewed through layers of glass,
Dust and rain spots?
This is not a waterfall, this is a picture of a waterfall,
I write above an empty space.

Empty Places

Sweet Friend

'I'm not an artist', you say.

'Why paint a thing that already exists?'

'And I'm not a photographer', you insist.

'Why take a photo when I can leave my house

And marvel at a tree, any time I wish?

'I can't create anything better than what already is,

I can't capture a moment and have it hold

In its flatness, an eternity felt.

'So, I'm not an artist.' You say.

'I'm not a photographer.' You insist.

'I can draw my thoughts so you can see them,

I can put an image to a word.

And you, sweet friend, can see what you like,

And feel your own eternity in its gaze.'

Empty Places

King of Pens

Tomorrow, the unpredictable tomorrow.

What sweet blessings, what sweet curses in disguise?

What lessons, what evolutions?

What integrations of a soul aligning with a soul?

Empty Places

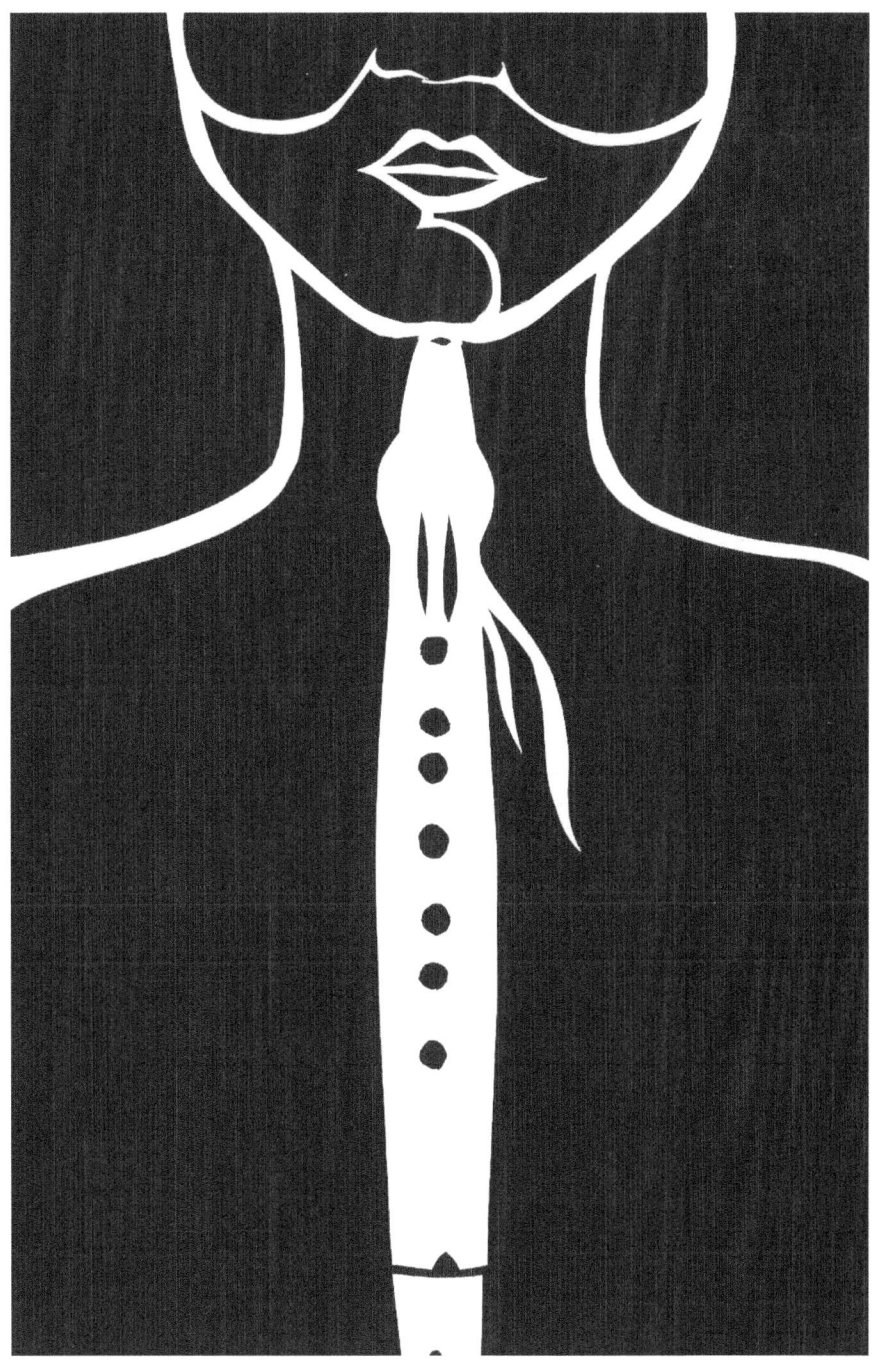

Words and Poets

When I have no words of my own, there is poetry.
When I find that speech has left me,
There is the words and wisdoms of others.
When I hear that voice in my head that says,
'Forget the distraction of poems,
And remember the important things of the world'
I do my best to ignore the safety net
That fear has wrapped around me, and remember,
Really remember,
That this expression of self has value.

Empty Places

Dad's Car

Lying in the backseat of dad's car,

Falling asleep to the passing coloured orbs.

Knowing that I'm completely safe with him,

Knowing that it's not safe to be myself with him,

Holding both these truths within me.

In this place I take things in,

Storing knowledge in my stomach and womb.

My wings melting into his footsteps,

I bubble apart.

I'm an echo of a man who's never known how to be.

But I know he will never let anything harm me.

But I know he can never protect me from himself.

Empty Places

Leave me Here

Anxiety crawls over my skin again,

All doubt and delusion.

My hands shake, my legs wobble,

I sway with the rotation of the Earth.

If I were to turn counter clockwise, I'd be turning the right way,

Every other movement is against.

At this time, my body is a seed,

I germinate within it.

I must be aware of what I nurture the soil around me with,

What I absorb at this time will be me.

So, I walk imaginary paths,

Sing off imaginary rooftops,

Get into deep conversations with beings in my head.

He makes me a batch of nettle tea, and this is the beginning,

Not of something new, but of something old,

Something that has been a long time in coming.

'Did you hear the wind howling last night?'

Dust coats everything I touch.

There's too much to tell you, so I tell you nothing instead.

I drink my tea,

I try to blow the dust away,

It covers everything, including me.

I'm made of it,

A body of ashes waiting to scatter,

Waiting for a thumb to reach down and smear me.

'Drink your tea, let it warm you.

Feel the heat of the cup in your hands.

Breathe in the scent of cut grass and tousled earth.

Feel the low-lit sun through the lavender clouds.'

There's so much to tell him,

So, I tell him nothing,

And hope he knows, somewhere deep down,

What it is that I feel.

'Does the caged bird sing more beautifully than the free one?

Why does it stay even when the cage door is open?

Because it tells itself it's dangerous out there,

That there's safety in the known? No.

Because there's love in the cage, in the diminished self.

Because sometimes we'll willingly give up ourselves,

For the sake of a little love.'

Empty Places

In My Little World

Is there a sacredness in my silence?

In the firmness of my mouth staying shut?

The staples at my jaw,

Allowing for the intake of shallow breaths,

Would there be more to me if I removed them?

Would I find power in using my voice,

In the tightness around my lips softening?

Would it loosen the rest of me,

My throat, my shoulders,

The pressure around my heart?

What would I even do with a voice?

What song would I sing first?

Orange blossoms and geranium scent the air,

And I hear my voice like a chiming bell.

A little rusty from under use,

But as clear and as bright

As tumbling river water.

The sound of me vibrates in my chest,

And my heart glows and grows.

There're shadows of shame around

The wound of my voice,

Shadows that only use can dissipate.

My voice is a voice that only needs acceptance and love,

It's a voice that only others have told me is wrong.

Let me hear it over the drone of them,

Let me get used to it before I share it.

Empty Places

Be My Body

I know, I know, I know,
I am a body,
My soul is a caged bird.
I spread my wings and
Tattered are my feathers,
Bruised and torn against the bars.
I know, I know, I know,
I am the storm that howled all night,
That wrapped around this house
And wouldn't let go.
I battered at the windows,
Soaked through to the foundation,
Tried to lift myself out of this place,
And find myself across some rainbow,
With silver slippers on my feet.
I know, I know, I know,
This is just a dream I'm having,
A part in a play I'm rehearsing,
A V.R headset across my eyes,
Imagining the world into existence.
This time around I'm the caged bird,
And the cage, and the jailer, and the key.

I know, I know, I know,
I am a body.

"...souls are simply bound and glued in the body, and compelled to survey reality through the body as through a prison wall, instead of freely by themselves..." – Plato

Empty Places

Shibari

It's not the cold metal
It's the warmth of rope.
The marks across skin,
The burns on wrists,
The impressions braided into flesh.
It's not being restrained,
Locked in with chains or cuffs,
It's being held.
The comfort and freedom of restriction,
Of breath and body, thought and purpose.
It's being a balloon filled to burst with helium,
The rope as string and hand.
The unburdened self,
Free to go this way or that,
To explore the universe,
Without fear of spiralling out.
It's the safety of another's control,
And the tenderness of another's release.

Empty Places

It's not always damage…

My heart is yellow,

Canary's wings and a blackbird's beak.

It chirps like a cuckoo clock,

Jaws open like a mewling chick,

It's eyes, redcurrants, glistening with dew.

It lives in a nest of dried twigs and brown fur,

Its body is plump and round,

Quickly outgrowing its home.

It used to be an egg with a crack along the side,

And so scared of damage, caused and done,

I'd spend my time hiding,

Trying to patch up and repair.

So little of me understood that the moment

Before change is terrifying,

And that the breaks in our hearts,

Is where new life creeps through.

Empty Places

Séance

Shaking off my winter coat,

Snow and cold blusters and rolls from my body,

I become the muddy soil where things can grow.

From my hands spring small white flowers,

And around my eyes form black feathers.

My spine becomes a spiral,

A whirlwind of energy moving up and down,

That violently shakes and trembles my body,

As pulses leave my heart and womb.

The women open the window,

To let the old out,

Then burn frankincense and geranium,

To fill the empty places.

Somethings are a metaphor,

And somethings aren't,

With no one ever questioning which one is which.

Empty Places

Remind Me

Remind me again.

Remind me again why the colour of my skin matters,

What religion I am or am not,

What country I'm from.

Remind me again why my gender matters so much to you,

Whether I wear dresses or trousers, boxers or bikinis.

Remind me again why my body shape matters,

Its curves, its thickness, its petiteness, its thinness,

Leg length or shoe size.

Remind me again why looks matter,

Whether I shade my eyes or whiten my teeth,

Fill my lips or contour my cheeks.

Remind me again why your opinion matters more than mine,

Why your value, your status, your worth is more than mine.

Remind me again why your voice can be heard,

But silence is my best defence,

My submission, the easiest way out.

Remind me again, why you're free and I'm not,

Why you're exempt from a system that enslaves and consumes.

Remind me again, why I'm still not your equal.

Empty Places

Grandfather Clock

We made a deal,

You would speak the words into me,

I would live them out, a wound in my heart.

We made a deal,

You and I.

Before birth and suns,

Planets and bodies positioned above pool tables,

Before clocks struck twelve and twelve.

We would cut each other open,

And learn to live broken.

In between the wounds, the openings,

We rearranged the empty cups

And filled them up with lessons learned,

And lessons yet to.

As these things go,

For a while, we forgot,

That we made a deal,

In the dark we'd find a poison,

And use it to make ourselves stronger.

Empty Places

In the Infinity of a Wolf Moon

With weights tagged to my fingers
I step out, looking for a new adventure
A new journey to find myself on,
To lose myself on.
I burn old tarot cards as an offering
To the god of Sometimes, who tells me,
'Sometimes it's good to sacrifice for the things we want.'
In the wind, the ashes scatter
And with it I let fly disappointment and doubt,
The trickster on the road
That tells me to turn back.
And in my mind a door opens,
A promise of roses and their secrets,
A continuation of a journey already started
And the invitation of something new.
For now, I'll sit in the smoke of the past
And pretend my stillness isn't waiting.
I'll pretend its rest and a gathering of strength
And not a fear of change tangling around my feet.
'Work with me.' the universe breathes around me.
In the air I smell roses, raspberries and lemons.
In the glow of the moon, I see I'm almost there

And this is the start and not the end.

Empty Places

Should Have Started

I want the journey of a book of poetry,
I want the beauty of dreams.
I want the cuts to be shallow,
I want the lightness of touch,
The tincture on the skin,
The feel of cotton.
I want the burning in my lungs
As I run across worlds to find me,
And bring me home.
I want the glisten of a tarot card,
I want the bruise of lips.
I want the change of movement,
I want the bite to reach bone.
I want the life I could have had
And not the life I'm leading now.
I want the start and not the end,
I want the end to be the start.

Empty Places

A Thought in a Hundred Parts…

Thought 1: Let me explain. I don't talk… much.
Words are important, they have a sacred weight,
They can't be wasted on anything, on anyone.
On the label at the birth of The Word was:

'Use with care. Has the power to create gods, rewrite worlds, destroy and consume both the speaker and the listener'

When we speak it should be because we have something to say,
Something vital that can be expressed in no other form.
Anyone can speak and say nothing,
It requires little thought or skill or care.
So, I'll explain. I don't speak much. I write.
Writing requires us to think,
To do our best to make sure we are expressing ourselves,
Our thoughts, our ideas, in a concise, perfectly, imperfect manner.
Though this is another thought, for another time.

Thought 2: Do you know who you are?
This is an experience I had during a meditation:

I floated above the Earth, of which out from, were protruding giant beings who all resembled Morgue, looking like spokes on a mace, from a great blue football.

I saw myself as one of the many Morgues, watching over the Earth, and laughed.
I'm sure this was my mind explaining to me, in terms I could understand, that I know who I am, and I'm not alone.

Thought 3: I've always known who I am, forgetting has never been my problem.
Wanting to be other than what I am, has been my problem, wanting to be like everyone else.
My failures to fit has been my path to silence, my path to solitude and isolation.
In this isolation I found acceptance of myself.
With acceptance came downloads,
Concepts, information, knowledge, ideas.
Some so beyond me they would break me apart before reassembling me.

Thought 4: I had an idea to write my thoughts down in short bursts.
If you're reading this, you're investing your time.
A part of your mind is now thinking these thoughts.
Do you know why you're here?

Thought 5: When I was eighteen, I had a thought that began with a question:

'What is the meaning of life?'

So, I attempted to answer it.

Thought 6: To answer this question I created four characters,
Their names were Emma-O, Jnana, Sky and Anubis.
I created a world for them to live in,
Then asked them all the same question:

'What is the meaning of life?'

They went on journeys to find the answer.
I'm not saying they found anything.
It was the journey that was important.
The questioning of what's good, what's evil,
Right, wrong.
Is god real, or something we created?
How far could they push themselves to find out?

Thought 7: Creation comes easy to me.
Creating worlds in my head, creating people.
I learned a long time ago,
I'm not fully, completely, attached to this body.

I'm an idea, a concept.

I exist everywhere and anywhere.

Thought 8: This is one thought, split a hundred ways.

One thought, into another, then another…

These thoughts are me and are not.

These thoughts are a bridge,

The working title of a life.

I'm caught between wanting to share

And keep to myself.

You scare me.

I'm outside of your world,

I'm looking in.

Thought 9: Splitting my thoughts is frustrating.

I think too fast when I'm alone.

My mind only slows and stops when I'm in your world.

I wish I could download these thoughts.

Wouldn't you prefer that?

A download directly into your brain?

Or would that be too invasive?

Thought 10: I'm caught between the mundane and what I am.

You say I'm not what you expect.

Why would I give you what you expect?
I want to do what I love,
Not what's expected of me.

Thought 11: Can I lure you like a siren on a craggy rock into the middle of the ocean?

Thought 12: Would you understand me then?

Thought 13: I was born on Friday the 13th.
You say that's what makes me 'weird'.
I don't want normal, normal speech.

'How are you?'
'Interesting weather we're having.'
'I hear it's going to rain.'

If we talk, let's talk about something even more transitory than the weather.
If we talk, tell me what you're thinking.
Don't be normal.
Don't be like everyone else.
Don't almost touch something deep and true in the back of your mind,
Then scare and run away from it.

Thought 14: Is it possible to spread truth through fictions?

Thought 15: Is this fiction?

Thought 16: Birth is painful. We are being born.
This is a memory.

I'm seven.
I'm staying with my grandparents for the second time in my life.
It is here, in this place, in this memory, and the one adjoining it,
That I learn to be silent, to speak when spoken to,
To not ask questions out loud,
To do as I'm told.

Thought 17: Do it. Own it. Own the weird. Own your crazy. Own your madness.

Thought 18: This is the adjoining memory.

I'm five.
My favourite question is 'why?'
I can't change this about myself.
But they want me to.

Thought 19: Have you ever bought a book because you already knew what it would say?

Thought 20: You're never going to find me.

Thought 21: In this memory…

There is no such thing as curiosity in my grandparents' house.
At five years old I'm learning this.
Everything said has a consequence.
Every question asked, that is beyond my grandfather's ability to answer,
Is met with beratement, banishment from his presence and the rest of the family.
When he's done with me he'll turn on her.
How could my mother be raising such an awful child?
What was wrong with her?
Why wasn't she doing better?
And I'll listen.
She's humble.
She accepts his criticism.
Says she'll try to do better with me.
In the room I've been banished to,

She'll come and sit with me.

Explain that there are certain things I can't say or ask.

I should only speak around him when spoken to.

He has certain freedoms that we don't.

I don't ask why, but I want to.

It's my favourite question.

I had asked him 'why?'

Thought 22: I feel stuck.

I'm stuck in this body and the limitations that come with it.

This is a limitation.

Being in a female body is a limitation.

Beauty is a limitation.

Society is a limitation.

Females should be beautiful.

Being beautiful is the most enduring quality a female can have,

Beautiful and quiet.

Thought 23: Open the window. Please.

The air is sweet.

It brings inspiration.

Thought 24: Am I wasting time?

Is this a waste of time?

Am I wasting your time?

Thought 25: There's something enticing about the neutral body.
Designed to be anything,
But more alienating than classical,
A statement more than the neutrality in its name.
The neutral body is an ideal.
White. Masculine. Iconic. Perfect.

Thought 26: To be neutral, to be accessible to all, to be recognised, accepted,
Do I have to be white and male?
Aren't there enough of those?

Thought 27: I've always felt more androgynous than female,
Non-binary is the new word for it, my word.
This body is just a body, I'm not attached to it.
I'm much more mind than body.
Mind is genderless.

Thought 28: In my favourite bookstore there's a little section called:

'Black Writers'

I don't want anything I write to ever be in that section.

I don't want to be segregated.

My writing is not some great achievement on behalf of my race.

What they have seen as celebration is limitation.

Stop limiting me.

Thought 29: I didn't know if I would make it to thirty.

Thought 30: Where are you?

Thought 31: I've been taught to hate myself.

Why are women taught to hate themselves?

Why is it a birth right handed from mother to daughter?

Thought 32: Speeches:

'You have to wear bras, or you'll sag.'

'Don't frown, you'll get wrinkles.'

'Wearing make up makes you more attractive.'

'Watch what you eat, or you'll get fat.'

'Cover up.'

'Why are you always covered up?'

Thought 33: What would you say to your younger self?

Thought 34: Are you living the life you expected to live?

Thought 35: Are you following?

Thought 36: I first discovered Lilith in an astrology book, and I fell in love.
The woman rejected and punished for being herself.
She made more sense to me than Eve ever did.
I was a teenager and her rebellion spoke to me.
I thought I was bad.
I would steal bibles thinking it was ironic.

Thought 37: Deep down, I wanted to be normal,
But I couldn't find my way to that path.

Thought 38: Others tell us if we're good or bad,
It's not something we get to decide for ourselves.
Lilith didn't decide if she was good or bad,
It was decided for her.

Thought 39: Have I reached you yet?

Thought 40: You may have figured this out already,

Writing has been the only safe place in the universe for me.

It's a private space where no one can hear me,

But I can still say what I need to say.

Pick up a pen and begin to write.

Write your opinions.

Write your ideas.

Write your history.

Let your mind dance, unrestrained.

Thought 41: What have you done?

What have you emptied out?

It's okay to be awful.

Disobedience is the word tattooed on our bones.

You're a descendant of Lilith now,

Unclean,

Made from sediment and rock,

Slime, what was left behind.

You are god's afterthought.

Thought 42: I wasn't raised Catholic,

But I've always been aware that my family are Catholic,

It was the playlist in the background.

I couldn't be christened in the Catholic church,

So, I had to be christened at the local Christian church.

The Catholic church refused to christen the baby of a single mother,
Like my father leaving her had been her choice.
But she remained Catholic, and let me decide for myself.
At twelve I became a Wiccan.
She bought me my first book of spells.

Thought 43: I recognise three people from photos of my christening,
My mother, my grandmother, my uncle.
My godparents are in the photos,
But I don't know who they are,
They're strangers to me.

Thought 44: There's a dark undertone to all things.
We long to peek behind the black curtain and glimpse the other side.
We're drawn to horror, the darkness of reality,
The primal.
We're born in darkness and crave its return.
We want to know ourselves,
All of ourselves.
If you don't, why are you here?

Thought 45: Explore the world with me,
Without limits.

Thought 46: Silence has been my weapon,

Not just my defence,

An active, formidable weapon.

The things I know.

The things that would fall out of me if I ever opened my mouth.

Stop underestimating how much I can destroy your world.

Thought 47: Do I seem lifeless to you?

Are you bored yet?

I've been told I'm boring, that my existence is pointless.

I live in my head, and all my passion goes there,

Into worlds of my own creation,

Into the universe that resides within.

Thought 48: Are you someone I used to know?

Somebody that I used to know once told me that he wanted to see everything.

I said:

'I don't want to see everything; I want to know everything.'

He told me this was impossible.

He didn't understand.

I know that this life is finite.

It's not really about knowing everything.

It's about filling myself up with as much as possible before I die.

All he wanted to fill me with was himself.

Thought 49: What's the point?

What's the point of gathering, hoarding knowledge,

If I'm going to die and all of it will be lost?

It isn't.

Thought 50: Is this a milestone?

Is it around my neck?

Thought 51: I've heard it said that we are the first extinction proof species.

We're resourceful. We adapt.

I've heard it said that we've stopped evolving.

We've reached our biological potential and can advance no further.

I've heard it said that we're all becoming clones.

Are you all the same?

Thought 52: I've read that as cultures merge, we are becoming a monoculture.

I've read that diversity is disappearing.

Is this good?

No more war, no more bias, no more racism?

No more 'Black Writers' section?

Thought 53: Why are you here?

Thought 54: When I was born,

I knew exactly what I was going to write.

Do you believe that?

Thought 55: I didn't think I would make it to thirty.

When I was twenty-nine, I decided I wanted to die.

No one would miss me, no one would care.

Those who did, would realise, in time,

That everything was better without me.

Thought 56: I was prescribed anti-depressants.

Thought 57: I stopped taking them after a year and a half.

Not because I didn't need them.

I wasn't taking them for me.

I was taking them to make everyone around me feel better.

They weren't fixing me.

They didn't make life better.

I'm not someone people want to be around when I'm depressed.

My mouth opens, and worlds are destroyed.

I realised that this isn't my problem.

Thought 58: We want to know the unknowable.
When something is only partially revealed,
We seek to know more.
I want to know more.
I want to know everything.
Don't you?

Thought 59: Are you waiting for a sign?

Thought 60: Are you the master or the servant?

Thought 61: Are we living in accordance with our best selves?

Thought 62: Honest answers only.

Thought 63: My uncle once told me that the world seems out to get us because it is.

Thought 64: I'm telling you; the world is very simple, and very complicated.

Thought 65: What's the moral of this story?

Thought 66: I've never felt as though I have a history.
I'm not considered part of,
I'm separate.

Thought 67: Descendants of former slaves have no history,
No culture, nothing to call our own,
No base to build ourselves upon.
I tell myself this frees me.
I can be open to anything.
The whole of history is my history.
Any culture I want to taste is mine.

Thought 68: Women carry their stories inside themselves.
They tell their stories over and over in their minds,
Until they become embedded in bone and blood,
And passed on to their children.
These stories can empower or enrage.
They are the secret children,
Waiting to be born.
They rarely are.
Because of this,
The world remains the same.

Thought 69: There are things we're not supposed to talk about.
We have to pretend this is normal.

Thought 70: I don't belong in this world.
I don't fit its structure.
It isn't designed for me.

Thought 71: Step out of the society you didn't create and create your own.
We are fictional characters.
We are parodies of what we believe should be normal.
Everyone is a fiction.
We're just stories.

Thought 72: Wisdom is not something that comes with age,
It comes with questioning.
The best questions are the ones we're not supposed to ask.

Thought 73: Do you have any old family photos?

Thought 74: I don't. None that go past my grandparents.

Thought 75: Do you know your lineage?

Thought 76: I have a non-history.
It's in my blood.
It goes back generations impossible to trace,
Because slaves were not people,
They were cargo.
This non-identity reaches back,
And chokes us all going forward.

Thought 78: We are the clandestine battles won and lost.

Thought 79: I observe.
I absorb.
I soak in.
I want to be more.

Thought 80: We're getting closer.

Thought 81: In conversation with a bus driver:

'What do you do?'
'I'm a writer.'
'You don't get many black people who say that. Usually they're cleaners, or something like that.'

Thought 82: Are you even looking?

I'm right here.

I'm in front of you.

I'm behind you.

I'm right here.

Look.

Open your eyes.

Thought 83: I'm not hiding anymore.

Thought 84: The universe is a library.

In my dreams I visit this library often.

There's a stone altar the length of a human body in the centre.

Thought 85: This is a conversation we're having.

Thought 86: The whole world feels like a, pardon the metaphor,

A boy's club, to me.

A members only club.

I'm outside looking in.

The problem is,

I've accepted this as my place.

Thought 87: What's happening to you?

Thought 88: Are you still asleep?

Thought 89: My mother had five miscarriages and one stillbirth before she had me.
Does that make me her seventh child or her first, or both?

Thought 90: When she was pregnant with me, she was told I would have Down's Syndrome.
She was told to have an abortion.

Thought 91: She didn't, and I don't have Down's Syndrome.
What if she had listened to her doctor?

Thought 92: She's told me, often,
I wasn't meant to be born.
After five miscarriages,
One stillbirth,
Her doctor telling her to abort,
I was born three months early,
Attached to machines to keep me alive.

Thought 93: Have I internalised this?

Not meant to be born.
Don't belong here.
Never meant to be born.
Don't belong here.

Thought 94: I see you now.

Thought 95: Do you see me? Finally.

Thought 96: Then let me explain. I don't talk… much.
But I'm learning to.

Thought 97: The weight on our shoulders are wings waiting to come through.

Thought 98: I'm so much older than I think I am,
And so much younger too.

Thought 99: I'm older now then I was when I started this thought, fragmented.

Thought 100: Is this all any of us are?
A single thought, fragmented?

Empty Places

Empty Places

Empty Places

Printed in Dunstable, United Kingdom